The Nature Kid's Guide to
MONKEYS

DAVID ANDERSON

LP Media Inc. Publishing
Text copyright © 2026 by LP Media Inc.

For information address LP Media Inc. Publishing,
30012 Variolite St NW, Princeton MN 55371
www.lpmedia.org

Publication Data

Monkeys
The Nature Kid's Guide to Monkeys — First edition.

Summary: "Learn all about Monkeys, the Nature Kid Way"
— Provided by publisher.

ISBN: 979-8-89818-204-5

[1. Monkeys – Non-Fiction] I. Title.

Title: The Nature Kid's Guide to Monkeys

CONTENTS

MONKEY MYSTERIES

DID YOU KNOW?

A monkey named Miss Baker flew to space in 1959 and came back safely. She became a star!

Chatter! A monkey swings from tree to tree up high.

Monkeys are some of the liveliest, most fascinating animals on Earth. They live in forests, plains, and even snowy mountains.

Monkeys come in all shapes and sizes. Some are as small as a kitten. Others weigh as much as a second grader! All of them have nimble hands built for gripping branches, grabbing food, and getting into trouble.

There are over 260 kinds of monkeys in the world. Each one has its own tricks for finding food and staying safe. Some are colorful. Some are loud. Some will surprise you completely. Get ready to meet some of the wildest ones!

GRIPPING GREATNESS

A monkey's big toe works just like a thumb. It can grip a branch the same way your hand can!

Grab! A monkey wraps its long tail around a branch.

Monkey bodies are built for life in the trees. Their fingers wrap tight around branches. Their eyes face forward to judge how far a jump is. One wrong guess could mean a big fall!

Some monkeys have a special tail called a **prehensile** tail. It works like an extra hand. They can hang by it and grab food at the same time.

Monkeys have thick fur that keeps them warm or cool. Some have tough pads on their bottoms for sitting on hard branches all day. These pads never get sore!

BRILLIANT
BRAINS

Crack! A capuchin smashes a hard nut open with a rock.

Monkeys are some of the smartest animals around. They can learn new things and remember them for years. Some even use tools to get food.

Capuchin monkeys use heavy rocks to crack open nuts. Other monkeys use sticks to dig for bugs. They watch and copy each other, just like you learn from friends.

Baby monkeys learn by watching their moms, practicing how to find food and stay safe. A monkey's brain never stops working and growing.

Some monkeys can count! In tests, they always pick the pile with more treats.

TROOP TIES

DID YOU KNOW?
Monkeys remember who groomed them. They share food with their grooming buddies later!

Eeek! A monkey calls out to warn its troop of danger.

Most monkeys live in groups called **troops**. A troop can have just five members or over six hundred! They eat, play, and travel as a team.

Monkeys **groom** each other every day. They pick bits of dirt and bugs from fur. Grooming keeps them clean, but it also helps them make friends and feel calm.

When danger is near, monkeys call out loud. Different calls mean different things. One call might mean "snake!" while another means "eagle above!" A strong troop works together to stay safe.

HOWLING HEROES

Howler monkeys rest for up to 15 hours a day. Digesting tough leaves takes a lot of energy!

Roooar! A howler monkey's cry echoes through the forest.

Howler monkeys are the loudest land animals on Earth. Their calls can be heard up to three miles away! A special hollow bone in their throat makes the sound so big.

Howlers live in the forests of Central and South America. They spend most of their time high in the trees. Leaves are their main food, so they never have to search far.

Howlers howl in the morning to tell other troops to stay away. It is their way of saying, "This spot is ours!" The forest rings with their roars at dawn.

TINY MARMOSET

Squeak! A tiny monkey fits right in the palm of a hand.

The pygmy marmoset is the smallest monkey in the world. It weighs only about 4 ounces—less than a stick of butter! These tiny monkeys live in the Amazon rain forest.

Pygmy marmosets chew tiny holes in tree bark. Sweet sap flows out, and they lap it up like syrup. This sticky treat is their favorite meal.

Even though they are small, they are quick and alert. They can turn their heads almost all the way around to spot danger. Nothing sneaks up on these little lookouts!

MAGNIFICENT MANDRILLS
DID YOU KNOW?
A group of mandrills is called a horde. One horde can have over 600 members!
16

Flash! A mandrill shows off its bright blue and red face.

Mandrills are the largest monkeys in the world. A big male can weigh over 70 pounds—as much as most 8 year-olds! They live in the rain forests of Africa.

Male mandrills have bright blue and red noses. The brighter the colors, the stronger the monkey. Females and babies have much plainer faces.

Mandrills walk on the ground most of the time. They dig for roots, fruits, and small bugs. Their strong arms and sharp eyes help them find food hidden in the forest floor.

FUN FACT!

A male proboscis monkey's nose never stops growing. Old males have the biggest noses of all!

Honk! A proboscis monkey makes a sound through its huge nose.

The proboscis monkey has one of the biggest noses of any animal. Males have long, floppy noses that hang past their mouths. This funny nose helps make their honking calls louder.

These monkeys live only on the island of Borneo in Southeast Asia. They stay close to rivers and swamps. Their toes have webs of skin for swimming, just like a duck!

Proboscis monkeys munch on leaves, seeds, and fruit. They have big round bellies to help break down tough food. Those pot bellies are a sign of good health.

SWINGING SPIDERS
DID YOU KNOW?
Spider monkeys do not have thumbs. Their four long fingers hook over branches like living hooks.

Whoosh! A spider monkey zips through the treetops with ease.

Spider monkeys are named for how they look when they hang. Their long arms, legs, and tail spread wide like a spider in a web!

These monkeys live in rain forests in Central and South America. They rarely come down to the ground. Instead, they swing from tree to tree, covering miles each day.

Spider monkeys eat mostly ripe fruit. They travel far to find the best trees. As they eat, seeds fall from their hands and grow into new trees. They are the forest's gardeners!

CLEVER
CAPUCHINS
FUN FACT!
Capuchin monkeys can learn to
trade tokens for treats!
22

Chomp! A capuchin monkey eats ripe fruit from the treetop.

Capuchin monkeys are known for being very clever. They live in forests across Central and South America. You may have seen them in movies and TV shows!

Capuchins eat fruits, nuts, bugs, and even small frogs. They search for food together as a team. When one finds a treat, others often follow to share.

These monkeys rub plants on their fur to keep bugs away. They are always finding new tricks to solve problems. Scientists love to study how their busy brains work.

SNOW SOAKERS

Splash! A snow monkey slides into a steamy hot spring.

Japanese macaques live farther north than almost any other monkey. They are also called snow monkeys. Thick fur keeps them warm in freezing winters.

In some parts of Japan, these monkeys soak in natural hot springs. They sit in the warm water while snow falls all around them. It is like a cozy bath on a cold day!

Snow monkeys also make snowballs just to play with them. When snow covers the ground, they eat bark, roots, and berries. These tough monkeys know how to survive the cold.

GOLDEN GUARDIANS

26

Crunch! A golden monkey munches on bark high in the mountains.

Golden snub-nosed monkeys live high in the mountains of China. Their thick golden fur keeps them warm in icy cold. Their flat little noses point up like tiny buttons.

These monkeys live in big groups. Some groups can have over 400 members! On cold nights, they hug close together to share warmth.

These monkeys eat tree bark, leaves, and lichen. They are rare and hard to find in the wild. Seeing one is a special treat for any nature lover.

MUSTACHE MONKEYS

FUN FACT!

Emperor tamarins are about the size of a squirrel. Most weigh less than a pound!

28

Chirp! A tiny monkey with a long white mustache peeks out.

The emperor tamarin is easy to spot. It has a long, white mustache that curls past its cheeks! It was named after a German emperor with a fancy mustache too.

These little monkeys live in the rain forests of South America. They hop through the trees looking for fruit, **sap**, and bugs. Their small size helps them reach food bigger monkeys cannot.

Emperor tamarins live in small family groups. Dads help carry babies on their backs. The whole family takes turns caring for the young ones.

SPEEDY SPRINTERS
FUN FACT!
Patas monkeys can go days without drinking water. They get moisture from the plants they eat.

Zoom! A patas monkey dashes across the open grassland.

The patas monkey is the fastest monkey on Earth. It can run up to 34 miles per hour! That is about as fast as a racehorse at full gallop.

Patas monkeys live on the flat grasslands of Africa. Unlike most monkeys, they spend a lot of time on the ground. Their long legs are built for speed, not climbing.

When danger comes, a patas monkey runs instead of climbing. Speed helps them escape from big cats and eagles. They are the sprinters of the monkey world!

GRASS GRAZERS

Geladas can flip their lips inside out to show their big teeth. It looks scary, but it is just a warning!

Chomp! A gelada sits in the grass, munching like a tiny cow.

Geladas are the only monkeys that eat mostly grass. They pluck blades of grass all day long. Their small, nimble fingers are perfect for this job.

These monkeys live only in the highlands of Ethiopia in Africa. At night, they sit on steep cliffs to stay safe. The cliffs are too hard for enemies to climb.

Geladas have a bright red patch of skin on their chests. Males show off this patch to look strong and brave. The redder the patch, the more powerful the gelada!

CRIMSON CANOPY

DID YOU KNOW?
Bald uakaris have the shortest tails of any monkey in the Americas. It's only about 6 inches long!

Rustle! A red-faced monkey peers down from the treetop.

The bald uakari might be the oddest looking monkey in the world. Its bright red face and nearly hairless head make it look like it forgot to put on sunscreen!

These unusual monkeys live deep in the Amazon rainforest, sticking to the treetops near rivers that flood each season. When the waters rise, they leap from tree to tree without ever touching the ground.

A bright red face means the uakari is healthy and strong. A pale face means something is wrong. Other uakaris notice, and will avoid a pale-faced monkey when choosing a mate.

SAVING MONKEYS

Crash! Another tree falls in a monkey's forest home.

Many monkeys are in danger today. People cut down forests to build roads and farms. When trees go away, monkeys lose their homes and food.

Some monkeys are very rare. The golden snub-nosed monkey lives in only a few mountain forests in China. Helpers work hard to keep those forests safe and plant new trees.

You can help monkeys too! Learn about them and share what you know. When people care, forests and monkeys can both be saved.

MARVELOUS MONKEYS

Monkeys and apes are not the same. The easiest way to tell them apart? Monkeys have tails, apes never do!

Whoop! Monkeys chatter and play in the warm morning sun.

Monkeys have so much to teach us. They stick together, care for each other, and solve problems as a team. Every troop is like one big, wild family.

From the tiny pygmy marmoset to the mighty mandrill, no two kinds of monkey are alike. They swing through canopies, wade through rivers, and call out across mountain valleys.

The more we learn about monkeys, the better we can protect them. Every forest saved is a home kept wild — and every kid who reads about them is one more person who can help.

GLOSSARY

troop
A group of monkeys that live and travel together

groom
To clean fur by picking out dirt and bugs

sap
Sticky liquid that flows inside trees

horde
A very large group, often used for mandrills

prehensile
A body part that can grip and wrap around things, like a monkey's tail